KEEP GOING

IF YOU CAN TAKE IT, YOU CAN MAKE IT

ROB NORMAN

Keep Going
If You can take it, You can make it

Copyright © 2022 by Rob Norman.

Paperback ISBN: 978-1-63812-294-40
Hardcover ISBN: 978-1-63812-501-3
Ebook ISBN: 978-1-63812-295-1

All rights reserved. No part in this book may be produced and transmitted in any form or by any means, electronic, or mechanical, including photocopying, recording, or by any information storage and retrieval system, without permission in writing from the copyright owner.

The views expressed in this work are solely those of the author and do not necessarily reflect the views of the publisher hereby disclaims any responsibility for them.

Published by Pen Culture Solutions   06/21/2022

Pen Culture Solutions
1-888-727-7204 (USA)
1-800-950-458 (Australia)
support@penculturesolutions.com

CONTENTS

Chapter 1 My Universal Laws of Life 1
Chapter 2 Suffering. Early Days 6
Chapter 3 Amateur Radio to the Rescue 12
Chapter 4 The Department of Defense 19
Chapter 5 A Psychiatrist, at last. 29
Chapter 6 A Suitable Job 35
Chapter 7 Building the Log Cabin 44
Chapter 8 A New Property 60
Chapter 9 Amateur Radio in the Outback 63
Chapter 10 Family and Friends 69
Chapter 11 Living according to Principles 83
Chapter 12 KEEP GOING 87

THIS BOOK IS DEDICATED TO MY UNIVERSAL LAWS OF LIFE.

The Expanding Universe is incomprehensibly vast and about 13.8 Billion years old while Our Planet Earth is around 4.5 Billion years old. There are roughly 400 Billion Stars in our Milky Way Galaxy alone and according to current estimates, about 2 Trillion Galaxies in Our Universe, not to mention the trillions and trillions of Planets, Suns, etc.. They say that there are more Stars in the Universe than grains of sand on Planet Earth. The circumference of the Earth is about 25,000 miles. High frequency Radio Waves, being electromagnetic radiations travel at the speed of light, about 186,000 miles per second, basically being received instantaneously around the World. Depending on the relative position of Mars from Earth, Radio Waves can take up to about 20 minutes to reach the Red Planet. The Space Craft Voyager 1 has been traveling away from Earth for over 40 years, having been launched in 1977. It's currently in interstellar space and over 13 Billion miles away. It's Radio Signals take something like 19 hours to reach Home. As we strengthen our influence in Space, due to the time delay in Radio Communications, a new form of Communication will need to be invented. In my opinion, this will involve Mental Telepathy or Quantum Communication. If we can befriend ourselves and then each other here on Planet Earth, then our destiny is out there exploring and discovering. Imagine for a moment, what this World of ours would be like without Radio Communications. They're vital to our way of life and without our current understanding of our place in the Universe which is largely due to Radio Communications, we would still be living in the 'dark ages'. Consider how dependent Defence Forces are on Radio Comms. Italian inventor and electrical engineer, Guglielmo Marconi is credited with the first transatlantic Telegraphic Radio Communications in 1901 and now the hobby of Amateur Radio has been around for well over 100 years. We stand on the shoulders of those who have gone before us and their hard work and contributions. It is apparent that Amateur Radio can be a gateway to the advancement of our Civilization. It's in our Nature to go beyond. Looking towards the future, we need to see over the horizon to the possibilities and the hope which is there. Developing Radio Systems can be Inspiring because it means that we will be able to do more than we currently can. Imagine for a moment the result of discovering and manufacturing the means with which satellites can use Radio Wave Technology to locate submarines under water. That Radio System itself could save our Democratic Way of Life. I feel that in times of future International Conflict, those Countries which can render ineffective Radio Communications of the Enemy, may be almost unassailable. Shielding of Radio and Electronic Circuitry is used extensively, but if a means of penetrating these shielding measures is brought into Reality, that very discovery may produce a decisive and crucial outcome. I should think that these measures are now, to a degree, a reality. Also, Remote Control of Amateur Radio Stations is a reality and Remote Control of advanced technologies in Space also require Radio Communications. The more aware we become of Space and what may be out there, the less self- centred we will be. TV programs such as 'Star Trek' and 'Star Wars' help in this regard. As we slowly further Our Reach into Space, Radio Communications of one form or another will help us to broaden our horizons and we will realize, if we survive long enough, how insignificant we are in the grand scheme of things. 'Looking back we can see that our Planet is just a pale blue dot in an ocean of darkness.' Perhaps one day with this more expansive view of our insignificance, we will be able to see more clearly how futile it is not to work together and we may then gradually leave conflict behind. We are all really 'Children of the Universe' and subject to It's Universal Laws of Life. The consequences of our expansion into Space would mean that Radio Communications could Save Our Civilization because without it we would feel as though we were the Centre of the Universe, not knowing the vastness beyond and we would not be able to leave our home Planet Earth. Radio Communications always have been and always will be a means of Humanity Expanding, learning the Truth and moving Forward. They are Vital.

It is easier said than done.
Courage is moving through the pain and fear.

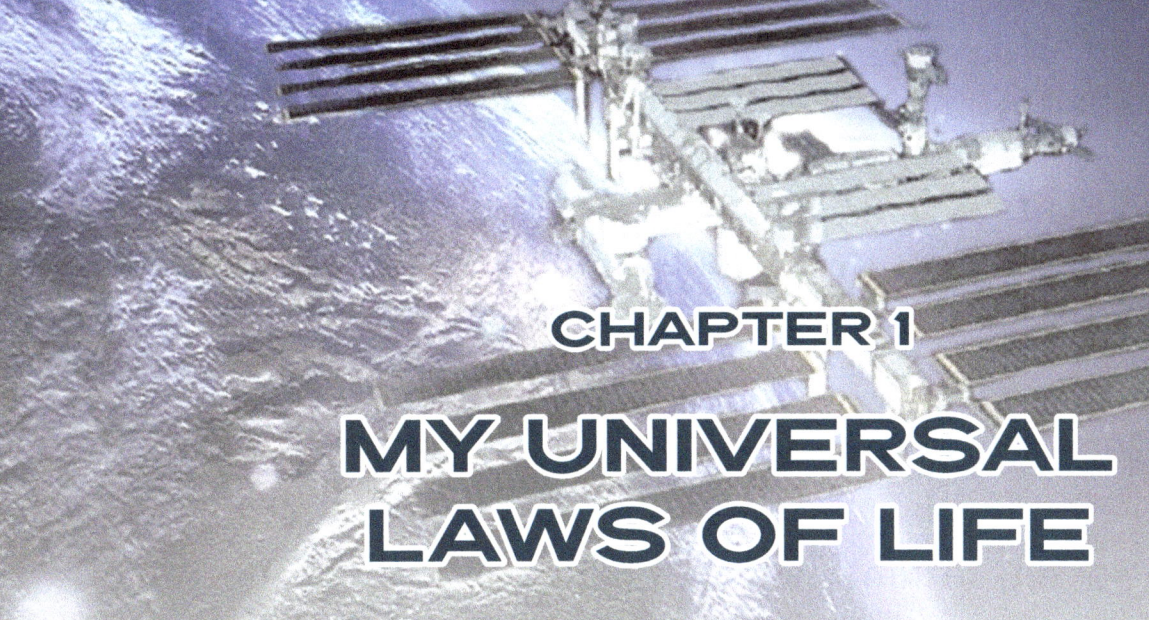

CHAPTER 1
MY UNIVERSAL LAWS OF LIFE

Suffering. I don't like it either.

But if we persevere with that suffering, it has the potential to help us in the long run. If we are willing to KEEP GOING, there may appear a light at the end of the tunnel, or signs of one form or another which can be our guiding lights to follow and persist, no matter the struggle. These tailormade signs have meanings for You as an individual. When mentally unstable it is often difficult to see the signs or understand the meanings, but never the less, KEEP GOING.

You see, we are much more than we believe ourselves to be.

You, being the same as me, have incredible staying power. Our problem is that we don't realize how fabulous we are and therefore fall way short of our potential. Your Self Belief is nowhere near where it needs to be for You to be consciously what it is that You really are. Excellence, Perfection, Fabulousness. That is the pathway needed for You to follow so that You are headed in the right direction. If You are on the wrong pathway, then it can be like hitting Your head against a brick wall and not knowing what else to do. It doesn't and will not do You any good. You need to firstly plant Your feet firmly on the right path.

I have found over many years that we need to learn how to like ourselves. Yes, learn how to. In my case, when I was a teenager, my struggles were severe with a mental illness called Schizophrenia. A lifelong problem. It was horrendous and I understand that many of us face problems of one kind or another and I hope that this short book may help You to firstly, understand that You are much more than the problem You are facing.

I used to hate myself because I could not be the person I wanted to be. The person whom my parents had brought me up to be. Self hatred and anger were my default feelings in those turbulent dark days. But I didn't give up and neither should You because over the horizon and beyond those feelings, if You keep to the path, are good times where the sun has broken through the clouds and Your feelings have lifted. What I mean by 'keep to the path' is keep in step with reality which the Universe helps and supports because that path is real and works. I am talking about Principles, Values, Qualities. Universal Principles of Truth.

What I am trying to do in this book is to illuminate the direction in which You need to go towards health and happiness. These Principles and Values are as old as time itself and are real. Integrity, Freedom, Peace, Individuality, Perseverance, Selflessness and many more. If these types of Principles are in the person, then that person can be great. If the Principles are in the people of a country, then that country can be great. Can I put it this way, although it may sound strange, but the Principles are in the DNA of the Universe and therefore in

You and me too. Therefore, these Principles are real, true and work. We are talking about Human Nature which is Universal and that which We all share, no matter our individual outward appearance.

If You are not going in the right direction, well, perhaps this book can help.

The image shows my sister Sandra and I long before the roof fell in on me, so to speak. But before we discuss this further, I am going to introduce the hobby of Amateur Radio now, as it played a large part in my ability to persevere over a long period of time despite the mental trauma.

Firstly, it is a hobby whereby licensed people can chat via Radio to one another Worldwide by voice and many other modes of communication too. These days my Amateur Radio Station is in the country and about 100 miles from where I live in the city. It is Solar Powered and Operated Remotely via the Internet from home. In other words, even though I live in the city, my Radio reception and transmitted signal takes place from our country property but is controlled from home.

For a better introduction to the hobby, please purchase my 'Introduction book' in either ebook kindle or paperback formats. A page has been dedicated to introducing You to the hobby on my website too. VK5SW.com

When I was 15 years of age, I read a book from my high school library called 'An introduction to Electronics.' I cannot remember the Author but she wrote a chapter or more about a young boy in the US who lived next door to a young Amateur Radio Operator and their eventual friendship and his introduction to the hobby.

This book inspired me as books can do.

On some weekends, my friend 'Lee' and I, at the time, used to ride our push bikes to the local rubbish tip and we would walk over the huge piles and mounds of rubbish and debris looking for interesting bits and pieces. He lived across the road from me. Having been reading the inspiring book, my attention was then tuned towards electronic devices or anything similar.

Over the next few weeks, tripping and at times crashing and falling, I eventually found an old shortwave radio partly covered by rubbish, because the glass of the old vacuum tubes reflected light, hitting me in the eyes and bringing my attention to it. Stumbling towards it, I eventually saw that it didn't have a cover and that the chassis was exposed to the weather. I hoped that it still worked and if not, how was I to fix it.

Loading it onto the back carrier of my push bike and riding a couple of miles to get back home was hard work. Lee riding behind, kept his eyes on the radio to ensure that it didn't fall off and during the following days and after tinkering for hours with it in my bedroom, this shortwave radio eventually worked. With the addition of a beat frequency oscillator to resolve the single sideband signals and a length of copper wire as an antenna, I was then able to receive and listen to Amateur Radio Operators from around the World chatting with each other. This is how 50 years of my Amateur Radio hobby began. At this time, I determined to become an Electronics Engineer and worked hard towards that goal.

In year 12 of high school, a fellow student by the name of 'Peter' worked with his father of a weekend as a bricklayer's laborer. I asked him if I could work with them too as a laborer. It was hard work but when young you have lots of energy and you can just about run until You drop.

CHAPTER 2
SUFFERING. EARLY DAYS.

Well, it wasn't the work that forced me to 'drop' but the onset of my mental illness. It came on like a ton of bricks towards the end of year 12 and about 3 weeks from the final exams for the year, I hit the brick wall. Prior to the job of bricklayer's laborer, I had also worked part time in the school holidays with my Mum who, at the time was a seamstress. Our neighbor, Mrs. Barker who did the same work as Mum, got her the job. They made material mattresses on their sewing machines to fit on top of outdoor recliner sun lounges. My job was to stuff the mattresses with small pieces of foam. I thought of myself as 'a mattress stuffer.' That job was a thing of the past now too. I became obsessed with a sore on the top of my hand and worried about it nonstop. I tried to cut it out with a knife but to no avail. This shows the state of mind. Study alone was difficult but by pushing myself to the limit to compensate for my mental illness, it got to the stage where I simply had to just stop. I could no longer study in any form and so when the six exams of my final year took place, my preparations were lacking, to say the least, having not opened a book for three weeks.

However, my results were not as bad as I thought they would be. I had enough points to study Electronics Engineering at the Institute of Technology in Adelaide. So, I registered and started the course, my parents having paid the fees. Catching the bus into and out of the city each day was difficult. Suffice to say that with my mental illness in full force, my feelings were horrendous. Feelings of fear and anxiety. My confidence and self esteem were rock bottom too and this continued for many years. I had feelings of hopelessness and shame for my inabilities to achieve. Everything I had to do was done despite my feelings. The feelings were telling me to run away but I never did. Sitting in the canteen, having a meal with others was terrifying too. After the first term of the course which was three months, it was obvious that I had no hope of passing exams because I was so concerned with my fearful feelings that I could not concentrate and take in the lessons at all and therefore would not be able to pass exams. So, I left. When I look back at these days and compare them to my life nowadays, my response is, 'thank Goodness I did not give up,' because where I am now is a good place to be.

In those early days, my main mental illness concerned feelings of fear/anxiety. I was terrified to the bone and found it difficult to do anything. These awful feelings were paralyzing. Happiness was nowhere in sight. Far from it. That word was never in my head. My fear concerned others and what they may think of me and it was difficult just to be in the same room with other people as silly as it may sound. I was hyper alert as if on a knife's edge. A sharp noise would take me to the ceiling, or so it felt. I felt ashamed that I had these feelings because my Mum and Dad had brought me up to be strong and independent. Instead, I felt weak and frightened and I always blamed and hated myself. This was a mental paranoid problem with which I struggled for many, many years. I did see my local Doctor once in a while but it didn't make much difference. This was a long time ago, but these days, if You have any emotional problems, please see Your General Practitioner who can refer You to someone who can help You. Please do that. I just had to keep going, no matter what. Fear is on the crest of the wave anticipating something awful is about to happen. Now I hear them say that all fear has as its origin, the fear of physical death. In those days, fear of others and my relationships to them, although irrational, reigned supreme, rendering me unable to find any enjoyment in anything at all. Total confusion reigned for years. The guilt and shame were soul destroying. It is easier said than done. Courage is moving through the pain and fear.

At that time, my Aunty Jean knew someone who worked for a bank and asked if I could have an interview with the prospect of working for them. I was considering a job as a lighthouse keeper because I thought that I would be isolated and able to do the job well and I was also thinking of applying to be a pilot in the air force but neither of those ideas took off. I applied for the bank job and was accepted but found it extremely difficult and scary to the back teeth, of course. But none the less, I stuck to it until my probationary period of six months had elapsed. At that point we reevaluated my suitability for continuing in the job but the unanimous decision among us, including me was that I look for employment elsewhere.

At that stage I was 19 years of age. Of course, electronics was my greatest interest and so I applied to have an interview with the Department of Defense which, in those days was known here in Adelaide as The Weapons Research Establishment. WRE. The interview must have gone well and I was eventually told that even though my age was rather old to be an apprentice, they would take me on. I started my apprenticeship as a 'Radio Tradesman.'

And I found it horribly difficult. Anxiety, fear, guilt, shame and self hatred. My sleep patterns in those days must have been chronically out of whack. Feelings of anger were not what I wanted. I remember punching my fist into my bedroom door which broke through the surface and it's still there today. I didn't want to be this way. The problems I had at WRE were the same as usual, but I must stress though, that the people wherever I have worked have always been nice to me and it was in no way their fault that I was having problems. It was me, obviously. Those feelings were always awful wherever the social situation. Even though I liked the subject matter of electronics, it was the same as it had been at the Institute of Technology. I was unable to recognize and feel anything but discomfort. My perceptions were badly diminished as my negative feelings influenced every activity. For example, I could not talk to people. Too scared. The thoughts were unable to come to mind to chat to someone. Instead of being friendly and open as I would have liked to have been and had been brought up to be, I was cut off and isolated, in every way. I lived with my parents and they supported me as much as they could but I did not talk to them much about my problems. I could not do that easily. For one thing I did not want to upset my Mother in any way if I could help it and so I kept to myself. As with other people, I found it difficult to be with Mum and Dad and so I spent much of my time in my bedroom reading. I did play some sport of a weekend which I enjoyed. Tennis and football. I had been the captain of the football team in primary school and I found that just handling a ball such as throwing it against a wall and catching it, gave some pleasure and I do that to this day. So, I recommend that You turn off Your computer and phone some of the time and get outside in Nature. It can help Your mental health. I remember at one time playing tennis for a club on a Saturday morning where I happened to meet an old school chum whom I had played tennis with at high school. Here he was playing against me for another team. The striking memory which

I have of that day, is when I went out to my car in the street to get something. It was an old Datsun car and just across the road from me was my friend who had just climbed into his brand new blue Volvo. He was an electrical engineer for the Government and had gone to University when I had started my electronics course at the Institute of Technology. It was a depressing incident to see how well he had done in life and how unfortunate I had been.

CHAPTER 3
AMATEUR RADIO TO THE RESCUE

But for me there had always been Amateur Radio.

One of the magazines which I read in the early days in my bedroom was published by the 'Wireless Institute of Australia,' called 'Amateur Radio.' It is still in publication today in the electronic format. The WIA is the Australian Amateur Radio Organisation. Wia.org.au

Amateur Radio - Worldwide Radio Communications

I joined the association by sending off a cheque through the mail. Somewhat different to today's methods of payment. So, the magazine arrived in my letterbox every month and I was able to keep in touch with the current happenings in Amateur Radio. Above all else, I wanted to become a licensed Amateur Radio Operator. Even though talking to people, for me, was difficult. None the less, I pushed ahead despite this problem and bought books about the hobby which would, I hoped, help me to reach a level of understanding of Radio Communications to pass exams to qualify for an Amateur Radio Operator's license. There was a relentless drivenness in me to do this, no matter what. And so I studied and studied. What I wanted, more than anything was to be able to talk to Operators around the World. Not just locally. The idea of doing this was a driving force which pushed me towards that goal, whether I wanted it or not, really. I had to succeed. In those days, there were two classes of licenses. A limited and a full license. The limited only allowed operation on VHF/UHF bands of frequencies which usually meant local communication. I wanted the full license though which enabled one to operate on all bands and modes. This gives theapabilityy of worldwide communication. But way back then, you also needed to be able to both receive and send morse code at a speed of 10 words a minute. A few years before then, 14wpm was mandatory.

So, I built a small audio oscillator made using transistors and purchased a secondhand morse code key from a disposals store in Adelaide. And thus the journey into morse code began.

Practice makes perfect. I was a conscientious person and so gave it my best to be able to receive and transmit morse code, or CW, at

10wpm or better. This did, to a degree lessen my mental problems, because now I had a goal which I was determined to achieve.

Not only did I have to achieve this goal but I also had to know technical aspects to radio communications and also the rules relating to radio communications with other Amateurs. These two exams also had to be passed to qualify. I think the pass mark in those days was 70% but I am unsure now.

These days, there are a variety of Amateur Radio examinations needed to qualify for different grades of licenses. Young people can now participate in the Hobby because of the simpler grades of licenses. Girls and Boys around 8 years of age or so can qualify and then chat to other 'Hams.' Amateur Radio is also known as 'Ham Radio.'

I had bought Ham Radio books and publications with which to improve my knowledge. I studied as best I could by myself without help and without attending any classes. I was self taught.

Having practiced sending and receiving Morse Code for some months and being driven to learn about the technical aspects of Amateur Radio and the rules of operating, at last I felt that I was ready to sit for these four examinations. My mental problems were not going to prevent me from doing this. That drive was always there.

The examinations were held in the city of Adelaide at the Postmaster General's Office. I sat for the four exams and passed them all, first go.

This is the Power of Passion. Doing what You Love to do. Your Dream with perseverance can become reality. Thank Goodness for our Democratic way of life. Democracies are founded on the type of

Principles which we are talking about. Australia is the lucky country. Right. Now, onward and upward. Let's go.

My Morse Code Hand Key in those Days.

In the winter of 1970, I received through the mail my Full Amateur Radio License number SA 688, dated 8th June, 1970. My Amateur Radio callsign which they had assigned was 'VK5SW.' Countries around the World have different prefixes to their Amateur Radio callsigns. The prefix for New Zealand, for example is ZL, for England it can be G. The prefix of a North American callsign maybe N or K. Some Countries have more than one prefix to choose from. So, my callsign, VK5SW indicates that I am in Australia and the figure 5 means that I am in the state of South Australia while my individual letters are 'SW.' Having qualified, Worldwide Radio Communication was now possible for me. This is what I had dreamed of.

The right path that we were discussing earlier is the Path of Principles. We admire honesty, determination, selflessness, courageous struggle, helping others and our mates, just to name a few. These qualities and many more are supported by the Universe. This is the way It wants Us to be. This may sound rather up in the air, but this is the way things are. If You live qualities such as these, then eventually, the Universe can and will help You. But You need to be on the lookout and quite often, especially when we are mentally depleted, it is difficult to see what is happening around us. But don't give up though, KEEP GOING. Even though it is impossible to see at present, over that horizon, things are brighter. Like the sun coming up. When it's night time here, on the other side of the World, it's daytime. The sun is always shining, no matter how You are feeling. Sometimes it's hard to see that or be aware of it. We are each and every One the Heart of the Hero and the Power is in the Principle.

If this way of thinking about Principles isn't for You, fair enough. Let it go. You will anyway. We each need to find ways of feeling comfortable and I am not talking about drugs or alcohol but ways of viewing the World and Ourselves so that we have a threshold of comfort which helps us to navigate life. Not everyone is comfortable with the idea of Universal Principles of Truth and that's ok. We all need to live our life no matter how we may view it.

Prior to having qualified as a fully licensed Amateur Radio Operator, my Dad and I had added an extension to his tool shed which was in our backyard. We made the extension out of galvanized iron, the same as the tool shed and the same size, 12 feet by 7 feet. It was in this extension that I started to build my Amateur Radio Shack and talk to the World.

CHAPTER 4
THE DEPARTMENT OF DEFENSE

I was working at the Defense Department when I had sat for my Ham Radio exams. Once the extension was up and we had poured the concrete floor, I hurriedly wanted to get on air, so I borrowed money from the bank and bought my first Amateur Radio Transceiver which is both a receiver and transmitter. In those days, that radio used glass valves and was manufactured in Japan. Here in Australia it was known as the FT200. In the US, Tempo One was the name given to it.

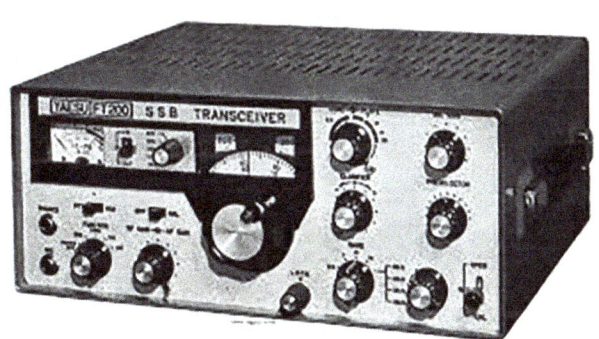

The transmitted RF output was about 100 watts and I used both phone, speaking with a microphone and also morse code. Over the future years I built and bought many morse code oscillators, bugs and fully automatic keyers. Preprogramed messages can be sent with the click of a button. Morse Code (CW) is such that You need to concentrate on what You are doing and this was always a challenge because of my mental problem which impedes the ability to concentrate. Both receiving and sending. These days we can do this with our computers which print out the received text signal on the screen and transmit our morse code message when typing too.

The antennas used here then were basic but allowed me to chat with Hams in Australia and New Zealand.

The Radio can be seen here with the cover removed. Believe it or not, despite my mental challenges, I built a 3 inch cathode ray oscilloscope which had been featured in the local 'Electronics Australia' magazine. I had bent up the aluminium chassis too. It can be seen above. This was in 1970 when I was 19 years of age.

Initially, speaking over the air was difficult. I'm sure many people around the world find this to be the case. But I knew that I had to push myself to do it, no matter what. The sound of my voice though was hard to push out when initially speaking into the microphone but by doing it, despite how I felt, I was over time, able to enjoy myself for once in my life. It gave me a sense of enjoyment which nothing else had been able to do and it provided a sanctuary away from my mental misery. I will never forget my first conversation on Amateur Radio. I remember it so well because of the kindness extended to me by a Ham in Western Australia, VK6 land. I am not sure of his name now, although I think it was 'Les' but he lived in a place called 'Como.' His callsign, I think was VK6MO. I explained to him that this was my first conversation and he set about to Welcome me to the Amateur Radio Bands and put me at ease by his manner of friendliness. I appreciated it very much and it remains one of the best contacts I have ever had and the memory of it will go with me to the grave. I doubt that he would have remembered it for long, but for me, I certainly have and here I am 50 years on, telling the World about it. This is the Power of Kindness. The Principle. At that time, I also made a Radio Friend in 'Les, VK5LC.' He was reliably on the 20 Metre band at the frequency of 14.110 Mhz. He lived in a nearby suburb and we often chatted. At one time, he invited me around for lunch with his wife and had asked if I would climb his radio tower in their back yard and adjust his antenna. He was a retired farmer and I was in my early twenties. I climbed his tower and adjusted the antenna. While there, he showed me an antenna which he had built and which was now on the ground. He called it a ZL special. I agreed to buy it and it was delivered in due course on the back of a semi trailer. The antenna was way too heavy. The image below shows it mounted on a tree stump. The pole above supported an omni directional multiband HF vertical antenna. The horizontal, rotatable antenna above the shed was used on 21 Megahertz to talk to Japanese Amateur Radio Operators. I also built the 4 element yagi antenna above the ZL special. It was used on 21Mhz too.

Over the months and years which followed, it was obvious that the antenna was too heavy and cumbersome to be of any value. It was heavy as lead. My brother in law, 'Greg' and I had brought home a 20 foot 4 legged tower on the back of his utility with the top of the tower jutting over the front of the car. I had spotted it in a cleared block of land, not far away. Having purchased it from the owner and brought it home, I dug the holes and Greg and I erected the tower and concreted into the ground. It was used to mount antennas.

In those days, I mainly operated on 14 Megahertz which is a frequency whereby, if the conditions of the Sun are conducive, you can chat to Amateurs Worldwide. As time went on, I gradually improved my Ham Shack by lining the walls, building benches and even pinning painted egg cartons to the ceiling to help reduce the echo effect when talking, although I don't think they made any difference.

This hobby gave me something which nothing else did. Pleasure. We are driven to be happy although it is hard to come by for many people. Me included in those days, especially. The Radio activity was able to help me to not think about my problems so much and this aspect helped me to KEEP GOING because now, there was always Amateur Radio there in the back of my mind which I could enjoy. It was a source of comfort. Something which previously, I didn't have. Work at the Defense Department was difficult too. Similar to my other jobs because the problem lay in me, not out there, nor in anyone else. But I kept at it though, as best I could. It is difficult to convey these feelings because the words are unable to go deep enough to elicit the feelings. Suffice to say that mental struggles like this are horrible, horrendous and isolating because most others are unable to feel your pain. I don't even know if anyone where I worked was aware of my terrible state. I never talked to anyone about it and when I went home, I spent most of my time in my Ham Shack down in the back yard. I was too uncomfortable, too on edge to be able to stay inside watching TV with my Mum and Dad. For one thing, I would not be able to concentrate on the TV and I wouldn't be able to sit still in their company. I just had to get away. And the same goes for having lunch at the Defense Dept. too. I couldn't sit with others in the cafeteria. I had to get away because of the intense anxiety, so I would drive my car to some lonely road on the Establishment and eat my sandwiches by myself. My memory is a little sketchy here but one time, we had a social occasion one Saturday night which I went to. I cannot remember the occasion well but in those days there were no drink driving rules and some how I found my way back home after the event but could not open the front door with my key because I was so drunk. Drinking helped to temporarily dampen the social anxiety. Anyway, when my parents arrived home that night after having been out, they found me sprawled out in the garden, dead to the world. Social anxiety is unpleasant, to say the least. At one time at home, I remember when we were having guests for Christmas Day, I left before anyone showed up and drove to a nearby town and booked myself into a caravan park for the night. I just could not face them because of the tremendous feelings of fear. Of course, if You have never felt these feelings, then these words are just words. I must have looked scared because the caravan attendant seemed to think I was weird. When Radio Wave Conditions allowed, I would often not come up into the house from my Ham Shack until after midnight. My time then was spent chatting to others in Europe on the short way for radio waves to travel around the World. North West from Australia. The antenna had to be pointed in that direction.

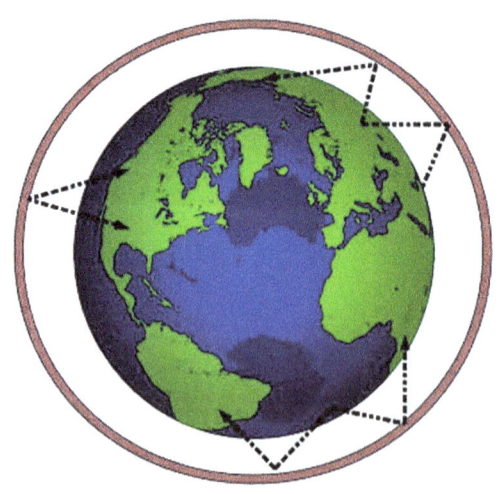

At that time, I bought a kit antenna from Queensland in NE Australia. It is called a Spider Quad antenna designed for the High Frequency bands. It was a difficult antenna to build requiring gluing sections of fibreglass poles together and stringing between them, copper wires of the correct lengths. The shape was maintained by fishing line between the two sides of the Quad. Although cumbersome too, it worked very well and enabled my radio signals to traverse the World. The height to the center was 33 feet. I think my Dad and Greg helped me to erect it.

I built many circuits and electronic equipment in those days. Ranging from stereo audio amplifiers, a small AR transmitter, receivers, GDO, RTTY tuning indicator and other Amateur Radio equipment. I think most of us build such electronics. For some, understanding how electronic circuitry work is a driving force.

It sounds as though this book is all about me but many people suffer problems in life and the intention of this book is to show how this individual was able to KEEP GOING, no matter what. The way this was achieved, as stated previously, was by adhering to Principles which my Mum and Dad had taught me and by which they lived too and their parents before them. Do the right thing as you know it to be and KEEP GOING. I also had the purpose in life to operate Amateur Radio which helped a great deal.

I persisted in working at the Department of Defense until the mental barriers were beyond endurance and then I had to go and see the gentleman who was responsible for the Apprentice School. I think his name was 'Mr. Roberts. I had always liked him and so I told him of my problems. However, I broke down and cried because it meant so much to me to be working there, but the emotional strain was beyond what I could endure now. I told him that I had to resign. He was understanding and I appreciated that. In response, he said that these days they don't send apprentices to Woomera but they would make an exception and send me there if that is what I wanted to do. Woomera is a rocket range in Outback Australia where they test rockets and so much more. But I knew it was no good my going because wherever I go, there I am. The problem was me, not the location. Well, he said, in that case we will let you to go to any laboratory you would like to on the Establishment here. Anywhere you like. I said, thanks. Well, how about the Antenna Range which is where they test Antenna Characteristics. In hindsight, I'm glad that I went there because I learnt a few things about antennas.

But of course, that did not last long either and so eventually I was forced to resign because of my horrible mental state. The people at our Defense Department had been terrific but unfortunately, my personal mental chaos prevented me from continuing. So, I left after having been there for 18 months which had taken a great deal of perseverance and then I saw a Psychiatrist.

I also operated radio teletype, firstly using a large mechanical teleprinter and reams of paper but it was very noisy and was eventually replaced by the Commodore 64, shown above.

CHAPTER 5
A PSYCHIATRIST, AT LAST.

When mentally ill, it could be said that we have a narrow bandwidth to our reception of outside stimuli. We need a broad bandwidth which enables us to take in more of that which is outside of our internal state. We need to see a wide picture, not a narrow picture. We could say that we need, as in antenna terminology, an omnidirectional input, rather than a narrow directional input. This is difficult to achieve when mentally unwell because our feelings are often overwhelming.

I had gone to see my local Doctor who then referred me to the Psychiatrist by the name of Dr. Weston. After telling him of my problems, he said that it would be a good idea if I came into their day center. He asked me how many half days a week I would like to come in for, to start with. I replied, how about two. He said, let's make it one. The number of days a week slowly increased as the months drew on. But when I commenced going there, I found that it consisted of a beautiful old two story building which, central to the bottom story, had a large and lovely old staircase leading up to a waiting room and various other medical practitioners' rooms above. Of course, at the time, I was completely unable to appreciate this building at all as my thoughts spun around in my head rendering me unable to see past my nose. Anyway, of a morning we would have a group meeting consisting of about seven or eight patients and a nurse who directed the flow of communication. We each were encouraged to talk about anything which was worrying us but I couldn't do that at the time as I was too scared. When I look back on those times, it is hard to believe that my life was so bad compared to the present day. Today is ok, yesterday was unbelievably bad. The group meeting usually lasted an hour and then we would have a coffee or tea in the sunroom or dining room. I found this distressing and hardly ever said a word. I simply couldn't. I also had a series of shock treatments where they placed a cap of electrical leads on my head while unconscious and fired electricity through the wires to try to help my condition. I was told that it could be likened to shaking salt laden electrical wires near the ocean. The idea being to 'clean the wires of salt.' Anyway, it did not work in my case. The workshop was located out the back of the huge house. It was a separate building where, after morning tea, we tried doing hand craft of one form or another. I remember, at one stage, I made a mosaic picture out of broken tiles. They also had a pottery wheel and some of the women patients would do sewing while the male patients tried their hand at woodwork among other activities. This was designed to help us to become used to people around us while engaged in various activities using our hands. I think this was my favorite activity there.

Dr. Weston had put me on medication which he felt would help me. It did slow me down and reduce the 'hyper on the edge feelings' but it also meant that my brain worked more slowly and tiredness was a constant companion. Initially, it was difficult to take the injections because the effect was such that, well, I can't really describe it. I became very sensitive. By that I mean that it felt as though my skin had been ripped off and I was exposed to any outside stimulus. It was a heightened state of awfulness to start with. Over time it gradually dulled my senses and mind. I had gone from hypersensitive to dumbed down. The correct dosage of medication was achieved over the coming weeks and months. However, for the next 50 years or so, my personality was deadened by the medication which was used in those days. It was basically like throwing a wet blanket over your entire brain. Loss of energy was one of the worst side effects for me. I had to push myself all the time to do things. You couldn't just jump up and act. It was more like saying to yourself, 'Come on, come on, get going.' It was not easy for me and no doubt not easy for any of the other patients there either. As you will see, my later life involved working physically, so the tiredness was a terrible ongoing problem for 40 odd years but this medication enabled me to survive. Without it, I could not survive. I would have had to have died. However, in 2017, my current Psychiatrist, Dr. Behrens, told me that they now had new medication on the market which may help me. As I said, the old medication knocked out most of the brain, whereas this new medication only targets certain overactive parts of the brain. He told me that my problem was caused by an excess of Dopamine. The neurotransmitters and receptors are dealing with too much of it which causes the perceptions to be unreliable. In other words, people with this problem are liable to hear or see or perceive that which is not real. An inability to see things clearly. At one stage, when unwell, I lost money on the Internet by trusting someone whom I should not have. My friends, family and Dr. Behrens came to my aid when they realized what was happening and put a stop to it. When mentally unwell with this type of disorder, it is difficult to see the way things are. You often believe things which are not true. It is only in the last 4 years that I have been able to be more like my real self, due to the new medication and the help I receive these days. By that I mean, realizing more of my potential. Smiling was not possible for me all my life until about twelve months ago, when that capability gradually awakened. It takes a long time when starting on new medication like this for it to level out and reach the optimum dosage. I will come back to this later in the book. Now, back to Dr. Weston 50 years ago who asked, if when I had finished at his day hospital and was well enough, would I like to go back and continue my employment with the Defense Department. I said, Yes please. He wrote them a letter and when they replied they said that it would be fine for me to come back and continue with them. At the time, I was happy to hear that. After some months at the clinic, I returned to WRE and commenced work there again, now taking the medication. But to no avail. I was only there a matter of months and had to resign again. I went back to Dr. Weston's day center and after a spell there of some months, he again wrote to the Defense Department asking if they would take me back. They did and after having been there for a few more months, I resigned and left for good. This was demoralizing but I never gave up living. In other words, I never, ever wanted to kill myself. I wasn't going to do that. For one thing, I would not do that to my Mum and Dad and for another, life is sacred, no matter what.

Amateur Radio was always there for me, as if waiting to throw its arms around me and give me a hug. It was a positive constant whereas other aspects of my life were negative. It is incredibly difficult to hang on when feeling horrendous. So, I would spend time in my Shack turning the tuning dial and listening and talking with people around the globe. It was, for me, always enjoyable and I want to stress this point. That being, if You are suffering, please look around to find something or some activity which may lift Your mood. A page on my website called 'Music Slideshows' may be able to help You. Also, I think being in nature, in whatever form, can help to do this because You are not looking at four walls within Your room. When outside, the visual terrain is different to being inside and it expands Your view. You are also using Your other senses too, although when mentally impaired, so are Your senses. But even so, You may hear sounds and other ways of taking in information of one kind or another. You may feel the wind, the glare of the sun. In other words, You are not as likely to spin around between Your ears. This is one of the important things to realize about life and that is when mentally troubled our perception is spinning around behind the eyes and between the ears. It is difficult to see past our noses but You need to see further afield and going outdoors encourages us to do so. I like to throw a ball against a wall outside and catch it. I did that when I was crook too and enjoyed doing it. So, get outside and look around. Maybe go down to the beach or up in the hills or wherever You like, so that You can stretch and expand Your view and take in something other than Yourself and Your worries. Perhaps take up walking, bike riding, running or other physical activities rather than mental activities. It may be a good idea to keep doing an activity regularly, like walking or perhaps do something with Your hands like using a saw, pliers, knitting needles, or painting or drawing but do it outside. Your creative capabilities are best when You are well, but despite Your capabilities at the time or the current state of Your mind, it is a good idea to do something which uses this faculty. It is not easy when ill but can help You none the less. Make things, like this book. Be creative. This way You may find something which grabs Your Imagination and enables You to lose Yourself in it.

CHAPTER 6
A SUITABLE JOB

Now, when it comes to the outdoors, my next and final job which I did for around 35 years was outdoor work. One of the aspects of outdoor work is that it is quite often hard work. This was the case with my job.

Working outdoors was my savior. It lessened my anxiety and fear of others dramatically. Being indoor with others increased these fearful feelings. In my case, I like using my hands so I was suited to this type of work too.

'Brush fences' as they are known here in Australia are constructed by weaving 'branches of a melaleuca' bush between wires which are tensioned. The melaleuca plants grow as a large bush in the outback areas and are cut down into branches which are tied together into 'bundles of brush.' The bush keeps growing and can be cut down again after about ten years. The brush fence can be made by hand as shown, or they can be packed by machine and the individual panels wired together to form the fence. But my physical work did not involve the mental stress that my mental problems created. The medication which I had to keep taking did enable me to function well enough to live a fairly comfortable life but the fatigue was always a problem and pushing myself physically to do the work took will power over and over again. We often had to dig post holes and concrete posts into the ground and pour a six inch concrete plinth or base for the brush to sit on. If interested, 'Hague,' my old boss and friend's website can be seen here. www.adrush.com

My Dad, 'Tom' did this work for most of his life too and when I had finished my time at the day center, I asked if I could come along and learn how to do it. Dad was reluctant for me to do this because he did not want his son to work so hard for so little return. Despite this he eventually agreed and so over the next few months he taught me how to do the job. But the most serious and near death experience I had was the first time I stopped taking my medication which was then in tablet form. After having done so, I eventually became desperate, so I had no choice but to ring Dr. Weston's rooms again. Usually the girls in the reception area answered the phone, but on this occasion Dr. Weston himself answered. This was a sign, the type of which I mentioned earlier. If he had not answered the phone that day, well it could have resulted in my death because he could tell instantly by my voice which was rock hard with no emotion, that I was catatonic, so he knew how to treat me. He made the appointment for about two hours' time. This is how the Universe works. Meaningful Occurrences which help You. My thinking at the time was that if he treated me badly without respect, then I would run through his window and crash to the ground from the second story. I couldn't have cared a less. Had that have happened and if he hadn't have answered the phone call, there would be no book here for You to read. When in such a mental state, a single word said by someone can be misconstrued and it can send you to the depths of hell. However, he treated me perfectly, showing nonverbal understanding and so over the next months I gradually took more and more tablets to calm me down again. This was extremely painful emotionally to start with as I mention further on in this book because it split me wide open with extreme discomfort. Initially, we started on a small dosage a day. Over the months, he gave me the tablets himself to make sure that there were no errors. That period was the worst of my life. Fortunately, I came through by the skin of my teeth. The feelings in such a state are beyond description. Your personality is blown to bits and all that there was of me then was 'The Will' and what I call 'The Skeleton.' The Will wanted The Skeleton to Keep Going and so It did. I don't think there could be a worse mental state than that because you are on the edge, liable to go either way. Towards life or towards death and you are not there because there is no you. It took many months but fortunately I survived and am now able to write this book about it, telling my story.

After working with Dad for a couple of years or so, he retired and so I looked around for a company to work for and found a new company and a new boss by the name of 'Greg.' He had a severe problem with anger and alcohol. He would often yell at his workers including me. A person with these problems would find it difficult to keep his workers, let alone run a successful business. When working for Greg, Dr. Weston employed me to erect a brush fence for him at his home which was in a leafy suburb of Adelaide. I am not sure how long I worked for Greg, possibly six months and then I left and approached another Brush Fencing company run by a chap named 'Hague.' I worked with him for many years and we became good friends. We were mates rather than boss and employee. He, of course, was a hard worker. He decided in the end to stop doing this sort of work, temporarily, and referred me to another Brush Fencing Company run by a chap by the name of 'Lynn.' He and I also became good mates and worked together for many years too. Both these men, hard workers were terrific to work for as they were lenient and allowed me flexibility which I am sure others would not. I am grateful for that and this helped me by taking the pressure off of having to finish building a fence by a certain time. We were all friends and I finished my working life with Lynn who kept his business going after I had left. I am so grateful that I had the good fortune to work for them. The picture shows us at a BBQ. Hague on the left and Lynn on the right with his wife, 'Tuula.' Me with the red shirt. I don't think that I ever told them of my mental trouble, present or past. We just kept working.

Throughout these years Amateur Radio was always a source of interest and enjoyment. I remember that I used to have a regular schedule after work with a chap in Japan who tried to teach me Japanese and I endeavored to teach English. It was on the 14Mhz band. My Ham shack was a place of refuge and comfort. When the rain pelted down on the iron roof, I loved listening to a station with my headphones on. A feeling of 'comfort' and 'all is well.'

Another station whom I talked to in those early days was a girl in Lima, Peru. It was on the 7Mhz band and we had a weekly sked and told each other what we had been up to. She worked as a nurse in a hospital. As well as chatting with each other, we also sent letters through the postal service. It was good to hear from her that way too. Different to these days of course.

In the earlier years of my illness, I didn't see my sister 'Sandra' and her family much as they moved over to Tasmania and lived in Hobart as 'Greg' my brother in law was posted there to work for his employer. So, they were unaware of my troubles with mental illness.

There were times when I really disliked the effects of the medication and I would go off the tablets which I was then taking. Mainly because of the drowsiness and lethargy caused by them. Having to work physically is hard enough without fighting against such difficult feelings. When I stopped taking the tablets, my life slowly but surely went down hill and I dragged others with me. There were three times which I can remember, where I stopped taking tablets. Each time, my family or Lisette would worry about me and then go and talk to my General Practitioner, Dr. Nora. One time, the mental health people sent an ambulance to take me into the hospital whether I wanted to or not. I stayed for months while they tried giving different medication. They never improved me until, as I said, about 4 years ago, the new high-tech tablets changed my life completely. From down and out for most of my life, to feelings of happiness at times now. My capabilities such as hand eye coordination, mental clarity, discernment, creativity, and many other abilities such as being able to talk and communicate well have become a part of me now. I hadn't been able to talk well for 50 years. The picture shows one such time. There were many times when it was difficult. Years of difficulty.

In my early forties, when working for Hague, I had to erect a color bond fence for a lady who lived near me. We rarely put up this kind of fence but I am glad that we built this one as I met my longtime friend 'Lisette' because of it. She owned the house and we started talking and I eventually asked her if she would like to go out with me. Well, she did, so we decided to go on a bush walk on a walking track not far away from where she lived. I only lived a few miles away with my parents. We have now been friends for 30 years or so. Not a passionate friendship by good friends. We still see each other quite often. She lives alone in her house and I live a couple of miles away, alone in my house.

SANFL Grand Final, 2018. Adelaide Oval. The 'Roosters' won!

When my Dad retired from putting up fences, he bought a pop top campervan and repaired it as he liked to work on engines and cars. Once road worthy, he and Mum took off to travel the roads of Australia.

I went with them on one trip. I had a small tent which I had to erect on the ground each night to sleep in. We travelled up the center of the country to Alice Springs.

Then onto a city called 'Broome' at the top end of the country. There we met Mum's brother and his son. We called Mum's brother, 'Uncle Van.' John the son had a boat and we went fishing each day and returned to the caravan park later in the day. The fishing up there is incredible. Huge fish such as Trevally, Barracuda, Tuna, Mackerel. Quite often 4 or 5 feet long. We caught more than we could eat, so the fish were filleted and frozen.

When in the boat on a calm day, we would see schools of tuna jumping up out of the water and turtles coming up to the surface which was flat as a pancake. Those images are burnt into my brain. We stayed in the caravan park for a week and then hit the road again by ourselves down the west coast of Australia. We called into many towns along the way and saw the huge submarine Low Frequency Antenna system just out of Exmouth. It was an interesting trip and good to see other parts of our country rather than just our home city. We were away for a total of 10 weeks. In Dad's retirement, Mum and Dad travelled all over Australia with their campervan. From South to North and everywhere in between.

CHAPTER 7
BUILDING THE LOG CABIN

Dad loved fishing so they quite often travelled to fishing towns nearby too. One such trip to a town called Marion Bay on Yorke Peninsula changed our lives. I drove over there to meet them in the caravan park where they were staying. A three hour drive, one way. The town was starting to be developed and vacant blocks of land were up for sale. One such block appealed to me and to cut a long story short, I borrowed some of the money from the bank and bought the block. It was a good size building block. Dad and I cleared the trees and bushes from the block of land and we firstly built a color bond shed in the back corner. We poured a concrete floor and that shed and the campervan soon became our home away from home.

I had always liked log cabins and thought about building one on the block. A company in Adelaide made log cabin kit homes, so I read their brochures and asked questions and eventually, Lisette offered to lend me money so that Dad and I could start quickly to buy and build the cabin. Dad by this time was getting on in age. With money I had saved and that which Lisette lent me, I purchased the kit home which was delivered in two truckloads. Dad and I jack hammered 40 holes through limestone and concreted 40 perma pine treated wooden stumps into the holes. Having cut the tops of the stumps level, we then built the steel chassis on top of them which supported the floor and house. Once we had done that and painted the steel again with rust preventative, Mum and Dad went home and Hague whom I was working for at the time and Perry a coworker came over for about three days in which time we erected the perma pine wooden panels around the perimeter of the house. They were each 4 feet wide and 8 feet high and heavy. It was now taking shape.

I screwed the color bond roof onto the roof trusses to keep the house dry. This type of activity was good for my mental health because it gave me a goal to achieve and with help, I did achieve it. Of course, I couldn't do it alone. I am grateful to everyone who helped me. I used an Amateur Radio over there too, having run copper wire as the antenna around the perimeter of the roof. Having built this house which had verandahs front and back, our lifestyles changed because we spent more time over there.

Innes National Park, nearby.

The completed Log Cabin.

After about a couple of years of working on it part time, the house had been completed. Mum and Dad and I had many happy years there. When Dad died, I rented it out on short term holiday rental. I called it 'Cosy Cabin.' Five years later I sold the house. It had been a terrific experience thanks to the help of my family and friends too. It took a lot of effort but I was repaid with the enjoyment of working with my Mum and Dad and the good times which we had there.

I bought a secondhand wooden boat which Dad and I repaired but it proved to be too heavy and cumbersome when at sea. We would often have barbecues in the shed or out in the back yard where Dad had built a brick barbecue.

Mum had done a lot of work on the interior of the house as well as the gardens. Lisette helped with curtains and carpets and many other aspects. We refurbished the kitchen which had been used in her sister 'Robin's' house and built it into the cabin. Building this log cabin was the biggest project we have ever attempted. I sold it about 10 years ago, I think. A month ago, March, 2021, I took my caravan over to Marion Bay and stayed at the caravan park for a couple of nights. When I went around to see our log cabin, I was totally surprised. It was no longer recognizable. The owners have completely renovated it but it is certainly much more modern than it used to be. A picture of it taken a month ago can be seen at the end of the following images.

KEEP GOING

51

What a surprise it was. For one thing, it is now painted white.

The end of the original log cabin's roof is visible at the back of the front addition. Much more modern now and talking to a chap 'Leon' who lives up the road, I was told that they have also built an entertaining area at the back of the house.

A page on my Website is dedicated to our 'Holiday House.' A short 3 minute video tour of the house can be seen at the bottom of the page.

A few months later I returned to Marion Bay with my Caravan in tow which was parked in Innes National Park close by and drove my car past our house again. I slowed down coming around the bend in the road and there in front of me was a woman walking from the house towards her parked car. I open my car door as I approached her and told her that my Dad and I had built the log cabin some years ago. 'Megan', the owner with her husband, was very friendly and took me inside to show me around this transformed house. This is the way the Universe works. Meaningful Occurrences which help You. Well, how do I describe the transformation. It was beautiful. White walls, clean lines, very modern and up to date design. At first I could not recognize the rooms but when we came to the lounge room, I could see that the layout was familiar but the materials used, instead of timber, were high class, modern and refreshing. Most materials were white in color and gave a feeling of spacious luxury. Her two blonde daughters were lovely too. I left feeling grateful to Megan for being so generous and friendly towards me. I wont forget that experience.

This book is about Self Belief.

I am trying to show You that Your predicament need not stop You from doing Your best to make Your life better, one way or another. What do You want in life? Do You know, or don't You.

You are much more than You believe Yourself to be. I will be repeating this throughout the book because it is our inability to recognize how terrific we are, which prevents us from being able to actualize it. You may feel inadequate or weak or unimportant and of no value to Yourself or anyone else, but the truth is the opposite. No matter what You look like or however unable You are, at Your core, You are the Hero. One of excellence, integrity, selflessness, friendliness, courage, perseverance, tenacity, never give upness, unruffled and much, much more. These are Universal Principles of Truth and You are That. The Hero. Self belief, Self Empowerment, the Power is in the Principle. These values, qualities are the truth of the matter and therefore they work. By work, I mean and I want to repeat it, the Power is in the Principle. If the Universe was not made this way with these values and principles, then they would not work, but they do. And they do because this is the way life is, because the Universe is this way. Always was and always will be. You are also this way and are influenced by the Character of the Universe. It is in Your DNA and supports that which is true and real. That being Qualities, Values and Principles of Integrity and Love. If You keep going through the valley of the shadow of death, the Universe will be there because You are there and It can help You through. Don't give up. It is on Your Side and It Loves You and if You live these Values then Your life will be better for it. So, think of other people and how You may be able to help them. Be friendly, start a conversation. Many of us would love someone to talk to who can understand us. They say that what we really want in Life, is the recognition from others of our Real Selves, which is Courage, Love and the Qualities of Perfection despite Our appearance. If You can see that in homeless people, for example, then You will be rewarded. If You can see through the exterior to the interior, then You can help people at the deepest level and that help will be effective for them. You don't need to say anything. You just need to know it and become it and that deep recognition will get through to them and comfort them. When Your knowing is to such a degree, You become those Principles and Your Personality on the conscious level reflects them. Holding in mind the possibility that people are perfect, will slightly open the door to truth for You. Forgiveness indicates that You can realize that life is difficult for us all and that quite often we do things, the consequences of which we are not aware of at the time. Forgiveness to my way of thinking, is compassion for the difficulties of human life. If You live such Qualities and Principles then the Universe can come to Your door and open You up. It's DNA is in You and Everything else. Align Yourself, Your Thinking and Actions with the Qualities of the Universe. They are the Universal Principles of Truth and Your life will slowly improve because You are now living the way the Universe wants You to and so It can and will now be more able to help You. The more like the Universe You become consciously, the more Your life will change for the better because this is what It wants of You. We are slowly changing for the better.

At present, this is the way I see of changing Yourself to Become what You are meant to be. I think it goes something like this.

Firstly, You need to be aware of how and what You are thinking and most of us are not. So, to improve this aspect of our selves, take up meditation or some means of becoming Self aware. You need to know how You think and why. I meditated for some years and it helped.

Once You can do that, then You need to challenge negative thinking and question it. So, You want to go from negative to positive with Your thoughts.

Your attitudes and belief systems cause Your feelings and they are unconscious and automatic. Apparently, it's not just Your belief systems causing Your feelings, but the degree of attachment to them. If Your feelings are bad, You need to change Your thinking and beliefs but first, You need to know what they are and then challenge and change them. You change them by challenging them. This is not easy but we learn as we go and gradually improve.

So, let me sum it up now.

We think good thoughts. We change our negative beliefs by repeatedly challenging negativity and replacing with positivity. We eventually come to know that our thoughts of positivity are right and true. Eventually we become those attitudes, principles, values. The person we develop into is one of kindness, love, courage, determination, strength and many more positive values, qualities. Such a person has a positive effect on people and circumstances no matter where they may be. You become more Universal. As You slowly become more like the Universe and slowly take on its qualities, You become more capable, loving and influential. You will find that people like You because You reflect more love one way or another. It is Your Birthright. I also like to think of it this way. We try to make conscious that which is unconscious thereby reducing the amount that is unconscious. More is then conscious. When less is unconscious, our conscious awareness is expanded and deeper, closer to the Soul or Universal Unconscious. Because of this, more of the qualities of the Soul become conscious in us. We do this by living the Values and Principles. Universal Principles of Truth.

As I said, this book is about Self Belief, Self Empowerment. Most of us are not aware of what it is that we are but we go towards that which is done well. For example, You may like a particular song, or the way a football team plays their sport, or possibly a good book which You enjoy. What I am illustrating is that we gravitate to what is good or well done and that is because we ourselves at our core are perfect and excellent already and we want to get closer to that. Those things which are done well appeal to us and our society celebrates excellence. That is what You are. You know that unconsciously but not consciously. So, You need to become more aware of how fabulous You always are and always have been and You need to become that consciously. If You become more like the way You are in Your center, You will consciously improve in all aspects. You will become more fulfilled, satisfied, loving. The Universe Loves You. It is Love and so are You but You need to become that consciously. Then You will be more of Your True Nature. The Universe is Human Nature. You will become more Super. Superman or Superwoman or Superchild with greater Capability. I don't mean that You can fly or lift the Earth on Your shoulder. For example, one aspect being that Your creativity will improve because You are heading in the positive direction. Positive means that it adds, becomes more, whereas negative means it subtracts, becomes less. Real, true is positive. Unreal, false is negative. I think Life, to a degree is learning what Life is about and I hope this book can be summed up in one line. That being, Self Belief. Self Empowerment. 'You are much more than You believe Yourself to be' but not everyone is comfortable with this. If this is so for You, just let it go.

Again, these Principles, Values and Qualities are True and therefore the Universe is under them, supporting them and they are Positive.

They basically push You up in a positive direction. I mean that Your thoughts, deeds, actions, etc. pile on top of one another, underpinned by the Universe and supported by It. Therefore You become stronger because Your day to day thoughts, words, deeds add to Your strength of Personality since the Universe is the foundation on which You are built. You are building Your Character. Whereas, principles and values which are not real such as anger, selfishness, deceit, abuse, etc. are made by our thinking. The Universe can only support those qualities which are real. Those which are negative and not real are not there in the first place and because the Universe cannot support them, they go down or sink and collapse with negative consequences. They take You down with them. There being no foundation under them to build You up because they just do not exist and therefore cannot be supported. The Universe is positive, not negative. It is Loving. You need to be positive, not negative. You are positive and always have been at the deepest level but You need to become more consciously positive. You as an individual need to become consciously more like the Universe which can do everything and You and I are made of it. Love is It's core and Yours too. We need to see a big picture, not a small one. Suffering causes Us eventually to understand what we are made of. It takes courage among other great qualities to KEEP GOING in the face of oppression of one form or another. We learn that we are terrific and we come to know that we have been suffering badly. I mean we can see Ourselves and Our suffering from a distance after some time. 50 years between the ears, behind the eyes, unable to see past our nose. We gradually come clear of the turmoil and have compassion for Ourselves. We then realize that others suffer too and we grow compassion towards them. We have a greater degree of Self Love. When someone is angry at You for example, instead of reacting negatively, You understand their feeling and show them that understanding in Your behavior towards them which may be keeping quiet while they rave on. Or You may ask questions which convey Your Understanding. Try and see the events from the other's point of view and not just Your own. This takes practice and is often difficult. Compassion can change the World.

I can see that I am repeating myself, but I don't mind because I want to help You and these Principles do that. We are here to help each other to be the best we can be. Therein lies fulfillment. As I said, as You KEEP GOING in the right direction, some people, animals, birds, You may notice, like You more than they used to because they know how You feel about them.

I will come back to this line of thought towards the end of the book.

CHAPTER 8
A NEW PROPERTY

After having sold our holiday house, we purchased a block of land next to my sister and brother in laws' block out in the arid countryside about 100 miles away from where we lived in the city. Both blocks are about 450 acres each. The surrounding area is desolate and barren. Red dirt, kangaroos, emus, wombats and a bush which loves the harsh conditions called 'Blue Bush.' It covers the landscape. A year or two later, my brother in law 'Greg' and I cleared an area and built a large color bond shed on our new block. A concrete floor was soon poured and my Mum and I started to decorate the shed to make it habitable. I bought a gas fridge, stove and a wood heater for the cold winter months. Lisette had given me a large bed for the holiday house which we brought to the property and installed it into the shed. It was soon quite comfortable but in the extreme weather conditions, both winter and summer, it is too uncomfortable to be there. We used this for a getaway location but soon learnt that the weather had to be appropriate for us to go there and stay overnight.

To give us each independence, we bought an old caravan for Mum to sleep in. We parked it near the shed and my sister Sandra made it more comfortable by making curtains on her sewing machine which we hung in the van. We soon had a comfortable lifestyle there, although we didn't stay very long at a time. We designed the shed so that the two front doors opened to extend the length of the shed of a daytime. It meant that the front of the shed was open to the outside.

CHAPTER 9
AMATEUR RADIO IN THE OUTBACK

I soon started to set up an Amateur Radio station in the shed and so I bought a large 670AH lead acid battery to power the radios and lights. It has been in use now for 12 years. An 80 watt solar panel was mounted on the front of the shed to slowly charge the battery.

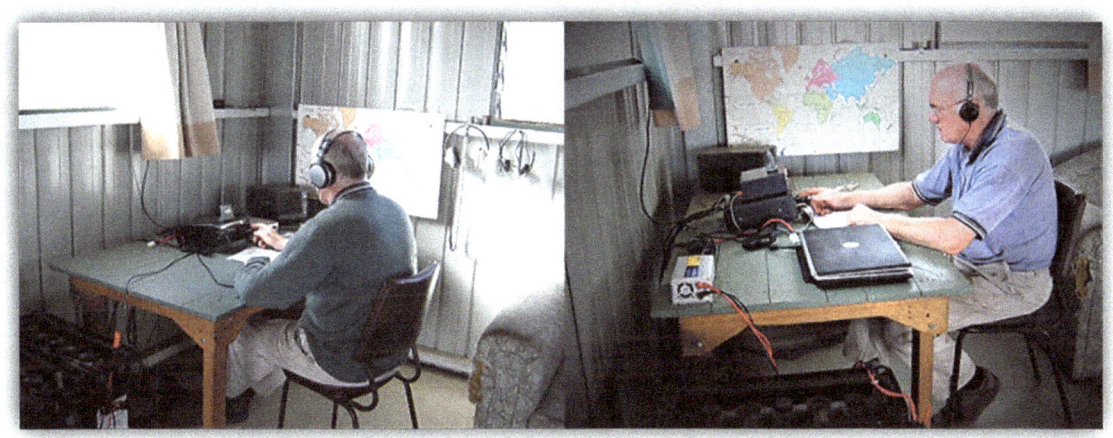

Over time I improved the shed and the Radio Station.

I constructed a number of High Frequency Antennas too and Sandra and Greg helped to erect them. Info and pictures of the Antennas are shown on my website.

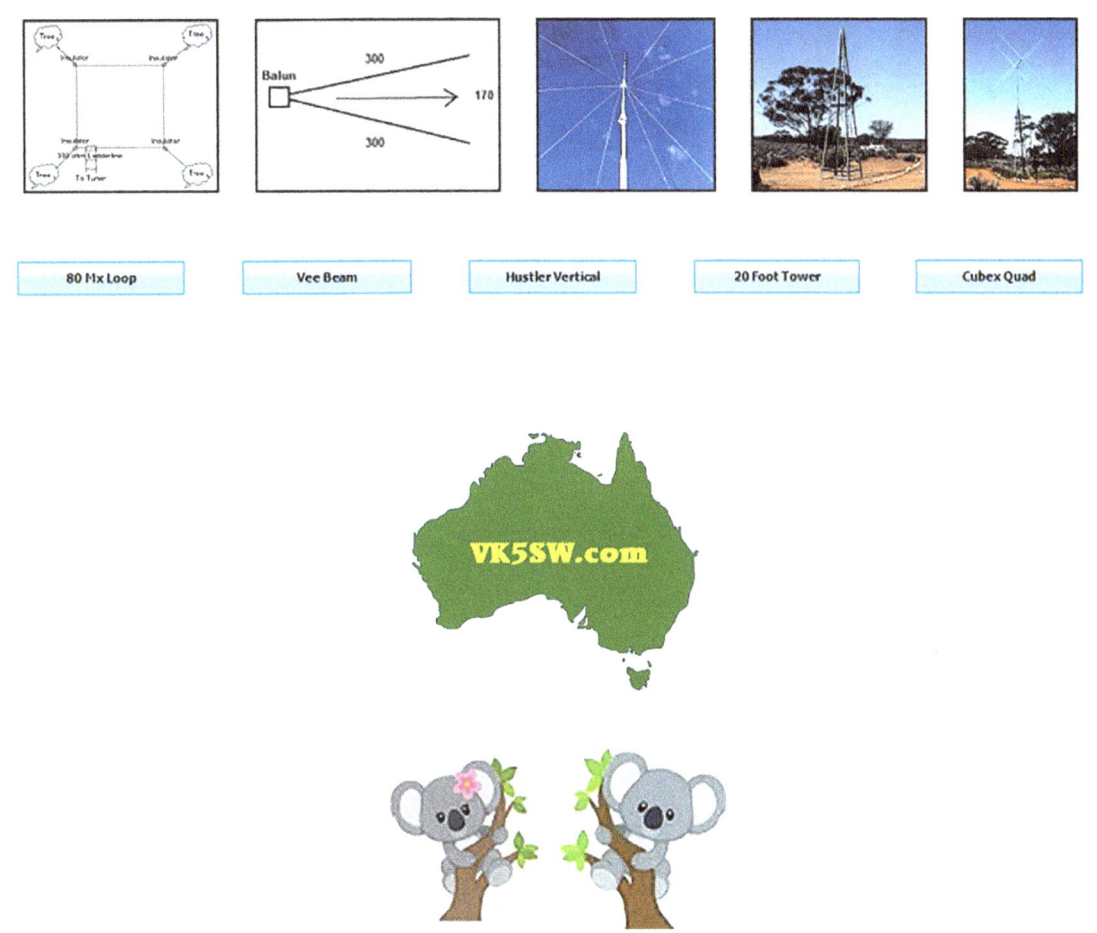

Australia, Down Under. Land of the Koala Bear.

Everything mentioned in this book can be seen on my Amateur Radio Website. www.VK5SW.com including HD Drone videos of the property and the 4 Solar Powered Amateur Radio Shacks. The page called 'Music Slideshows' can lift You up too.

Australia. Down Under. Land of the Kangaroo.

I also renovated an old caravan which was left on the property by the previous owners and turned it into a solar powered Amateur Radio Station.

I decided to build a new and smaller color bond shed too. This is another Amateur Radio Shack powered by the Sun.

CHAPTER 10
FAMILY AND FRIENDS

I want to add a few images of my family and friends here who have helped me throughout my life.

Firstly, my Mum, 'Edie,' who died recently at the age of nearly 95. She was Fabulous and had a good life. Always helped me through out, no matter what.

Mum's Parents whom we called 'Nanny and Grandpa.'
We usually visited them each Sunday morning
and have only Very Fond memories.

My Mum was in the Australian Land Army when a Young Woman and her brother, 'Ivan,' our 'Uncle Van' was in the Army's Special Forces in WW2.

Dad, 'Tom,' died some years ago and lived to the age of nearly 88. He loved playing golf and played all his life – to the end, when he used a small motorbike to help him get around the course.

He was always helping me with one thing or another. He liked to use his hands and build furniture or other useful items. He liked welding, woodwork and using his imagination to come up with something new to create and build.

He and Mum had a good marriage for over 50 years.

My sister Sandra and Greg, her husband, have been there for me just about all my life. When struggling with my mental health initially and needing to have my car repaired, I used to take it around to Greg who was usually able to fix it for me, free of charge.

Sandra and Greg have 2 daughters and 3 grandchildren. First Daughter Rebecca, Simon, Rebecca's husband. Their two Children, Ruby and Alex. Second Daughter Joanne, Son Elliot.

My good friend 'Lisette' has helped me constantly over the last 30 years. I'm grateful that she has been in my life.

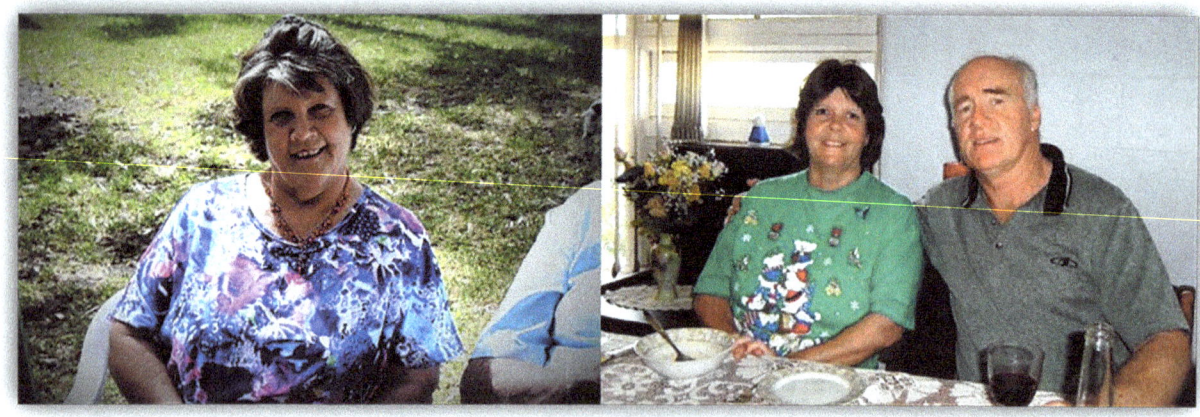

Her sisters Jeannie and Robin have been good friends too as has the rest of her family. Brenton, Guy, Hayley. Garry, Elke, Ava. At the time of writing, 'Pat' their mother is 97 and still lives alone in her own house. Lisette's father 'Ron' died some years ago.

I want to remind You of what I believe is the importance of being outdoors and not solely indoors on Your computer or phone. There is a feeling of freedom out there, especially if You can be in Nature without too much around You in the way of manmade buildings and objects. I understand that if You live in the city, then it is more difficult to find such places but it is desirable to do so. Perhaps go to the beach where there is space around You. In my opinion, it helps to take the pressure off the mind because it is surrounded by more space in these locations. That may sound silly but I believe it to be true. This feels right to me. Less psychological pressure and 'air pressure.'

Nowadays of course, with the advent of the Internet, our lives have radically changed. So it is with Amateur Radio too. I guess about five or six years ago I determined to be able to control my Solar Powered Amateur Radio Transceiver Remotely via the Internet. In other words, I can control the radio on the property from here at home, 100 miles away. But You can be thousands of miles away and providing You have a fast, reliable Internet connection, You can control Your Radio. For example, let's say You live in the U.S.A. and Your Radio station is in England. With the appropriate equipment and fast Internet connection Your signal is transmitted from England even though You are in the U.S.A.. Such is the power of the Internet. There are benefits in doing this too. Firstly, as in my case, the background noise level on the Radio at the property is dead quiet whereas in the city where I live, I can hear nothing at all on the Radio because of powerline interference, TV's and You name it. Also, large antennas can be installed at the property and thereby radio communications made more reliable. The following pictures show the Remote Radios setup at the property. Also, commercially run Remotely Controlled Amateur Radio Stations can be operated by licensed Amateurs.

My 2 element, 5 band HF Cubex Quad Antenna.
The height is 33 feet to the center.

In May 2021, I replaced the 670AH Lead Acid Battery which had been used for 12 years with no problems, with a total of 800AH Lithium Ion Batteries. The Lead Acid Battery needed to be topped up with distilled water every month or so but the Lithium Ion need no maintenance. They can be depleted by 100% and they keep their voltage high until the capacity is way down.

I also use 220AH Lithium Ion Batteries in my Caravan/Mobile setup. This is independent and isolated from the Car Battery.

The Radio used is the FT-450D and Diamond Whip Antennas.

The home location from where the Radio System on our property is Remotely Controlled via the Internet.

As I have said, Amateur Radio has helped me enormously. Through the thick and thin of my life, it has been the constant which I come back to time and time again. It has always been an enjoyable activity in my life and so I am indebted to the lady who wrote the book which initially inspired me and pointed me in this direction. So, thank You whoever You may be.

CHAPTER 11
LIVING ACCORDING TO PRINCIPLES

If you have a dream which You want to achieve, then imagine Yourself, right now having achieved it. Your imagination, Your thoughts have power and can bring that dream into reality. Of course, if You want to become a lawyer, dentist or whatever else it may be, then You need to knuckle down and work hard towards it. I think that the things in life which we treasure are those which we have worked hard to achieve. They show our Power and give a glimpse of what else we may be able to achieve. Justice will eventually prevail. I think that what we want is for others to tell us how good we are. Most of us don't do that but this book does. And it does so because You are much more than You believe Yourself to be. A Hero lies within You. When it comes to catastrophes in life, facts are not as important as the way we feel about them. The thoughts tend to go around in circles. We need to deal with our emotions. Cry if You want to. The pain comes from resisting the emotions, so we need to let them be and allow them to overwhelm us. Stay with them, don't resist but let them go on and they will gradually weaken. It is difficult. Guilt, depression, anger and many more will be in there but let them come and let them go. Please do not hurt anyone while doing this, including Yourself.

We are at the end of the book now, so I want to briefly mention the incredible Universe of Quantum Mechanics.

Quantum Mechanics these days can prove the truth of the Values and Principles in this book. Kinesiology or muscle testing also indicates Truth.

An overview, I think of Quantum Mechanics is the capability of a person to transform the mental into the physical. In other words, Your thoughts and feelings can and do change physical reality. Not because I say so, but because it is true.

The scientists talk in terms of the Heisenberg Uncertainty Principle, the collapsing of the wave front from potential to actual. From wave to particle. Particles can behave very strangely depending on the observer. In other words, the awareness of the observer changes the physical properties of the particle.

Professor Michelle Simmons who works at the University of New South Wales and won the 'Australian of the Year' award in 2018, is one such Scientist working with Quantum Physics. In her acceptance speech, she said that they are working and leading the world in trying to create Quantum Computers which deal with and endeavor to control individual atoms which is difficult. She said that if Quantum Computers can be built, then important problems within many fields of endeavor which now take hundreds of years to solve, will be solved in minutes. Science confirms that Your thoughts and feelings change Your reality.

An author whom I recommend is Professor David Hawkins. He died some years ago but his books and videos live on. Start with his book 'Success is for You.'

Happier days. My 70th.

My friend Lisette gave me a half hour helicopter flight over the Barossa Valley for my 70th Birthday. Fabulous. Up, up and away.

CHAPTER 12
KEEP GOING

We need to find a personal purpose. One or more. They will align with our values and who we are as a person and will possibly change over time. You always have a choice. A choice between the light and the dark. The pessimistic or the optimistic. It is often not easy but difficult. If You live these Values and Principles mentioned in this book, which are thought patterns of viewing and valuing Life, then Your Life can change for the better because the Universe is in tune with them. They are real and work. Always have, always will. They are the solid foundation upon which a 'bright and bubbly, rich and full life' can be built. Universal Principles of Truth are also the foundation upon which Great Democratic Countries are built and so it is for people too. We can each and everyone of us be a force for good. No one in my family knows what I have been through, until now because of this book.

Albert Einstein is quoted as saying, 'Two things inspire me to Awe. The Starry Heavens Above and the Moral Universe Within.'

I think Life is partly learning what Life is about. What is life and what does it mean. We are born and then start walking into the unknown. Each young person doesn't know what to expect. I think most of our problems are caused by ignorance but I don't think it's our fault. I think it's our Human Nature and Inheritance, but we can make our lives better though. Fear can be reduced by Accepting the Qualities of Humanhood which we all share. It is difficult to work life out, but as we grow and KEEP GOING, we learn lessons. That which You think is so important, probably isn't that important in the grand scheme of things, so come back and look around. Try to see from a broader perspective. Look up more than down. Don't get caught up in the detail. Look at the bigger picture. When we are immersed in our negativity, whether depression, anger, guilt and many more emotions, we cannot see through it. It is all encompassing but if You put Your attention on the horizon, then You can gradually come out of the fog. Provided Your feet are on the right path as given here and You live the Values and keep walking ahead, then that horizon can be like the Sun. Warm not cold, bright not dark and clarity not confusion. Think of the Horizon and keep looking at it.

Problems and trying times can make You Stronger and Wiser. 'A gem cannot be polished without friction, nor a man or woman perfected without trials.' Understanding can bring peace of mind. We initially don't know what is true and real but we are all in the same boat and there is more to You than meets the eye. We can Help Each Other by using our talents and capabilities for the Good of Us All. When We Help Others, We Help Ourselves. What this book amounts to is that You can change Your thoughts, feelings, attitudes and belief systems with effort. You can change Yourself and Your life for the better. Don't give up. KEEP GOING. It's a matter of being in tune with the way the Universe works. Live according to Universal Principles of Truth which include Integrity, Honesty, Love, Selflessness, Courage, Perseverance, Tenacity and many more Positive Qualities. As You live these Principles and Values, Your life will gradually improve because

You are becoming the Person the Universe wants You to be and It can support You. The Universe is always there but the problem is that You don't think about it. What I mean is that the Principles are always there but You are unaware of them.

And don't be afraid to Fail. The important thing is that You do Your Best and Honesty is the best Policy.

Great Democratic Countries of the World are Underpinned by These Values and Principles. Many, Many People have Fought and Died to Preserve Our Way of Life. Freedom is not Free. It has been Extremely 'Hard Won' and We are Eternally Grateful. 'The Spirit of the Anzacs Lives On and On. At the going down of the Sun and in the Morning, We will remember Them. Lest We Forget.' You are more than You believe Yourself to be and it is You who has the capability to change Your Life and Life around You because You are Fabulous and Precious whether You know it or not. The Universe made You so. It's in Your DNA. Use these Values and Principles to become the Personality You want to Be. It is often not easy but difficult. Courage is moving through the pain and fear. As You proceed along this Path, Life changes little by little from Black and White to Color. Your way of Thinking, Attitudes, Belief Systems, slowly, slowly change from 'What If' to 'So What.' From concerned to less concerned. From Pessimistic to more Optimistic because You are more in touch with the way things are. We don't see the World the way it is. We see the World the way We are. We need to Learn to Love and Feel Good about Ourselves.

So, come on Everyone, let's Go. Let's do some Good for the World and Ourselves.

Often it is a matter of trial and error.

Keep correcting Your mistakes.

Keep Listening, keep Learning,

keep Understanding, keep Creating, keep Loving and

Do Your Best and KEEP GOING.

Keep Going

Keep Going

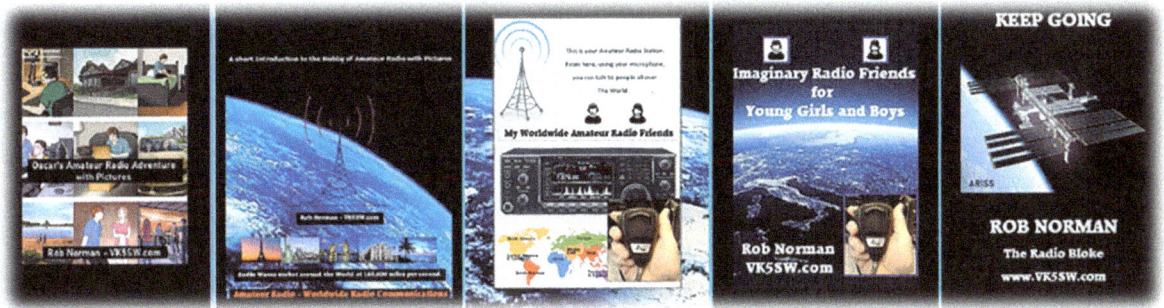

Rob Norman, Amazon.

Rob Norman VK5SW
www.VK5SW.com
An Australian Interactive Amateur Radio Website

**150 Videos and Music Slideshows which Rob has created.
Search ' vk5sw ' on You tube, Using Your Smart TV.**

LIFE LESSONS

Life on Earth teaches us Lessons.

'We are more than we have been and less than we hope to be.'

One foot in front of the other. One step at a time. Keep going.

'That which we persist in doing becomes easier, not that the nature of the task has changed, but our ability to do has increased.'

That which you think is so important, probably isn't that important in the grand scheme of things. So, come back and look around. Try to see from a broader perspective and don't get caught up in the detail.

Greatness comes from the heart. It starts with principles and values. Power lies in the principle. If the true Universal principles are in the person, then that person can be great. If those principles lie within the people of a country, that country can be great.

True universal principles work. False principles are not there and so cannot work. The universe cannot support something which is false and therefore not even there. False principles lead to negativity whereas Real Universal Principles of Truth lead to positivity.

False principles descend whereas True Principles ascend. False is negative, True is positive.

The deeper you can go when bad, the higher you can go when good. We see the world not as it is, but as we are.

It pays to keep it simple. A step in the right direction is a good step.

'Yesterday is history, tomorrow is mystery, so focus on today.'

Rob, www.VK5SW.com